I0460184

my personal

Countdown
to
Transition

~

Notebook
and Planner
for
Non-Retiring
Service Members

By International Best-Selling Author

United States Army
Chief Warrant Officer Five (CW5) - Retired
Combat Veteran

Dr. Sonya Howell Barrow

SONYA HOWELL BARROW

my personal

Countdown
to
Transition
~
Notebook
and Planner
for
Non-Retiring
Service Members

By International Best-Selling Author

United States Army
Chief Warrant Officer Five (CW5) - Retired
Combat Veteran

Dr. Sonya Howell Barrow

ISBN: 979-8-9923160-5-6
Printed in the United States of America

Cover design and graphics by:
Dr. Sonya Howell Barrow

The SoJaDe Group, LLC

Disclaimer

The content of this book is inspired by the author's own military experiences and is to assist non-retiring service members in strategically planning and organizing their transition to civilian life.

While the author shares personal insights based on her own personal experiences, please remember the objective of this book is to serves as an additional resource for transitioning service members.

The author encourages service members to consult with appropriate professionals, such as financial advisors, legal counselors, or career transition specialists for personalized guidance throughout their transition.

The use of this book implies the service member's understanding and acceptance of this disclaimer and his/her agreement to discharge the publisher and author from any and all claims or causes of action, known or unknown, arising out of the contents of this book.

The author hopes **"my personal Countdown to Transition ~ Notebook and Planner for Non-Retiring Service Members"** serves as a valuable resource, guiding towards a fulfilling and well-prepared transition.

i

my personal

Countdown
to
Transition

~

Notebook
and Planner
for
Non–Retiring
Service Members

By International Best–Selling Author

United States Army
Chief Warrant Officer Five (CW5) – Retired
Combat Veteran

Dr. Sonya Howell Barrow

Military Transition

Military transition refers to the process of shifting from active military service to civilian life. This transition encompasses various aspects of personal, professional, and financial adjustments that service members must navigate as they separate from the military.

It includes:

- **Career Transition:** Identify and secure potential future employment by effectively translating military skills and experiences into prospective civilian career opportunities, while acquiring new industry-relevant skills and certifications to maintain a competitive edge.

- **Financial Planning:** Managing changes in income, benefits, and budgeting for post-military life.

- **Healthcare and Benefits:** Transitioning from the military healthcare systems (such as TRICARE) to civilian healthcare or VA benefits.

- **Identity and Lifestyle Adjustments:** Adapting to a new daily routine, redefining purpose, and integrating into civilian society.

Military Transition

- **Family and Community Integration:** Helping to ensure a smooth transition for family members, finding new support systems, and adjusting to a different pace of life.

Military transition is a major life event that requires planning, adaptability, and access to resources to ensure a successful and fulfilling shift into civilian life.

Table Of Contents

A Letter To My
Fellow Service Member

Dear Fellow Service Member,

After serving over 26+ years in the U.S. Army (1992–2018) and retiring as a Chief Warrant Officer Five (CW5), I understand the unique challenges that come with transitioning from military to civilian life. Navigating changes in career, lifestyle, and personal identity can be overwhelming, especially for non-retiring service members who may not have access to the same resources as retiring service members.

Because of my own military transition experience, I decided to create, **"my personal Countdown to Transition ~ Notebook and Planner for Non-Retiring Service Members."** This guide offers a structured roadmap, breaking down the transition process into clear, actionable phases. It covers essential topics such as career planning, financial management, and personal well-being, aiming to empower you with the tools and insights needed for a successful transition.

While the **Transition Assistance Program (TAP)** or **Transition Readiness Program (TRP)** for your specific branch of the United States Armed Forces (Army, Navy, Air Force, Marine Corps, Coast Guard, and Space Force), provides valuable information, the sheer volume of material covered in a short timeframe can be overwhelming. Whether Active-Duty, Guard, or Reserve, this notebook and planner is designed to complement **TAP** / **TRP** by reinforcing key topics and offering a personalized approach to track your progress, set goals, and manage critical milestones—ensuring you remain organized and confident throughout your transition from military to civilian life.

No matter if you are 24-months or less from separation—be it **Voluntary** (such as Expiration Term of Service [ETS] or Early Release Program [ERP]), **Involuntary** (Medical, Administrative, Disciplinary, etc.), or other circumstances, this resource will guide you through each step, helping you navigate the complexities of civilian life with clarity and purpose.

Stay organized. Stay informed.
Embrace your next chapter with confidence.

Best Wishes,
Dr. Sonya Howell Barrow
United States Army
Chief Warrant Officer Five (CW5) - Retired
Combat Veteran
and
Amazon International Bestselling Author

my personal

Notebook and Planner
Belongs To:

_____

_____

my personal
24-Months (or less) Countdown to Transition

my personal
24-Months (or less) Countdown to Transition

The 24-months (or less) countdown helps to provide a method for navigating from active-duty military to civilian/veteran. By breaking down the process into manageable phases, it allows for early preparation for the service member, reducing last-minute stress and ensuring nothing important is overlooked.

The 24-months (or less) countdown is designed to give transitioning service members sufficient time, structure, and clarity to establish financial security, explore career options, and organize healthcare and family needs, all of which contribute to a smoother, more confident transition back into the civilian lifestyle.

The 24-months (or less) countdown establishes the foundation for a successful and fulfilling transition, helping service members enter their new chapter prepared and empowered with confidence.

Essential
Military Resources for
Transition Assistance

Essential Military Resources for Transition Assistance

Essential military resources are vital to successful transition planning. They provide the foundational tools and critical information needed to navigate the transition from military to civilian life.

- **Essential military resources are helpful with finding answers:** Service members are able to search for answers easier with minimal stress. This allows them to make informed decisions in a timely manner to ensure they approach their transition process with clarity and purpose.

- **Essential military resources serve as a guiding framework:** Service members are able to stay organized and focused while addressing the various complexities of planning their transition. Knowing where to turn for support instills confidence and it empowers service members to tackle challenges with ease.

- **Essential military resources provide long-term significance beyond the transition period:** Service members benefit from having a trustworthy set of tools and contacts at their fingertips whenever needed.

- **Essential military resources act as a roadmap:** Service members will receive the structure and guidance they need to successfully navigate their life-changing journey.

Essential Military Resources URLs

- **DoD Transition Assistance Program (TAP):** Provides information, tools, and training to ensure service members are prepared for the next step in civilian life.

  Website:
  https://www.dodtap.mil/

- **Veterans Administration (VA) Benefits Portal:** Access and manage your VA benefits and health care.

  Website:
  https://www.va.gov/

- **Military One Source:** Offers a wide range of resources for service members and their families, including financial counseling and transition assistance.

  Website:
  https://www.militaryonesource.mil/

- **eBenefits:** A portal for veterans to manage their benefits and access personalized information.
  ### Website:
  https://www.ebenefits.va.gov/

- **My Healthe Vet:** Access your VA health records, refill prescriptions, and communicate with your health care team.
  ### Website:
  https://www.myhealth.va.gov/

Phase 1
24 - 18 Months Prior to Transition

Creating Your Transition Foundation

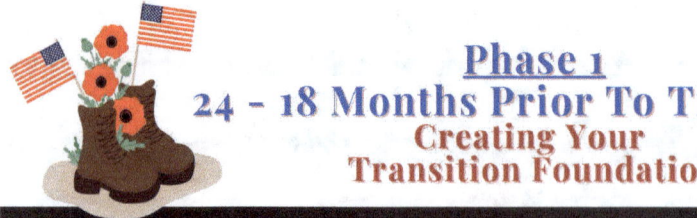

Phase 1
24 - 18 Months Prior To Transition
Creating Your
Transition Foundation

Phase 1 is about creating a transition foundation that provides stability, security, and confidence for your transition into civilian life. Establishing a very strong foundation during this phase paves the way for a smooth, fulfilling transition.

As you prepare for transition, here are a few specific things to consider 24 - 18 months prior:

- **Vision and Transition Goals:** Consider your vision. Define your transition goals and ideal post-military lifestyle. Consider where you'd like to live, future career aspirations, and family priorities.

- **Identify Benefits:** Now is the time to familiarize yourself with military benefits, GI Bill educational benefits, VA options and benefits, and healthcare plans.

- **Evaluate Finances:** Review your current finances. Identify all sources of income, expenses, and debts, and start building an emergency fund.

- **Skills and Career Assessment:** Access all of your transferable skills and explore career fields that align with your interests and experiences.

- **Preliminary Transition Budget:** Draft a preliminary transition budget with estimated income, benefits, and expected expenses.

The earlier you begin planning for your separation, the smoother the transition will be. Even if the timeline is uncertain, use this phase to build a strong foundation for your next chapter.

Month 24

Vision and Transition Goals

Identify Benefits

_____
_____
_____
_____
_____
_____
_____
_____
_____
_____
_____
_____
_____
_____
_____
_____
_____
_____

Evaluate Finances

Skills and Career Assessment

Preliminary Transition Budget

Notes

Estimated Budget
24 Months Prior to Transition

Fixed Expenses

_ _ _ _ _ Rent/Mortgage

_ _ _ _ _ Electricity

_ _ _ _ _ Water

_ _ _ _ _ Gas

_ _ _ _ _ Internet

_ _ _ _ _ Phone

Food

_ _ _ _ _ Groceries

_ _ _ _ _ Coffee

_ _ _ _ _ Snacks

Transportation

_ _ _ _ _ Fuel

_ _ _ _ _ Maintenance

_ _ _ _ _ Parking Fees

_ _ _ _ _ Insurance

_ _ _ _ _ Public Transport

Entertainment

_ _ _ _ _ Movies

_ _ _ _ _ Concerts/Events

_ _ _ _ _ Hobbies

_ _ _ _ _ Restaurants

_ _ _ _ _ Parties

_ _ _ _ _ Leisure Travel

Shopping

_ _ _ _ _ Clothes

_ _ _ _ _ Electronics

_ _ _ _ _ Beauty

_ _ _ _ _ Home Goods

_ _ _ _ _ Gifts

Medical

_ _ _ _ _ Doctor Visits

_ _ _ _ _ Medications

_ _ _ _ _ Health Insurance

Fitness

_ _ _ _ _ Gym Memberships

_ _ _ _ _ Sports Equipment

_ _ _ _ _ Wellness Products

Family & Education

_ _ _ _ _ Childcare

_ _ _ _ _ Tuition Fees

_ _ _ _ _ Books

_ _ _ _ _ Materials

_ _ _ _ _ Courses

Month 23

Vision and Transition Goals

_____

_____

_____

_____

_____

_____

_____

_____

_____

_____

_____

_____

_____

_____

_____

_____

_____

Identify Benefits

Evaluate Finances

Skills and Career Assessment

_____

_____

_____

_____

_____

_____

_____

_____

_____

_____

_____

_____

_____

_____

_____

_____

_____

_____

Preliminary
Transition Budget

Notes

Estimated Budget
23 Months Prior to Transition

Fixed Expenses

_____Rent/Mortgage

_____Electricity

_____Water

_____Gas

_____Internet

_____Phone

Food

_____Groceries

_____Coffee

_____Snacks

Transportation

_____Fuel

_____Maintenance

_____Parking Fees

_____Insurance

_____Public Transport

Entertainment

_____Movies

_____Concerts/Events

_____Hobbies

_____Restaurants

_____Parties

_____Leisure Travel

Shopping

_____Clothes

_____Electronics

_____Beauty

_____Home Goods

_____Gifts

Medical

_____Doctor Visits

_____Medications

_____Health Insurance

Fitness

_____Gym Memberships

_____Sports Equipment

_____Wellness Products

Family & Education

_____Childcare

_____Tuition Fees

_____Books

_____Materials

_____Courses

Month 22

Vision and
Transition Goals

Identify Benefits

Evaluate Finances

_____

_____

_____

_____

_____

_____

_____

_____

_____

_____

_____

_____

_____

_____

_____

_____

_____

_____

_____

_____

_____

Skills and
Career Assessment

Preliminary Transition Budget

_____
_____
_____
_____
_____
_____
_____
_____
_____
_____
_____
_____
_____
_____
_____
_____
_____

Notes

Estimated Budget
22 Months Prior to Transition

Fixed Expenses

_ _ _ _ _ Rent/Mortgage

_ _ _ _ _ Electricity

_ _ _ _ _ Water

_ _ _ _ _ Gas

_ _ _ _ _ Internet

_ _ _ _ _ Phone

Food

_ _ _ _ _ Groceries

_ _ _ _ _ Coffee

_ _ _ _ _ Snacks

Transportation

_ _ _ _ _ Fuel

_ _ _ _ _ Maintenance

_ _ _ _ _ Parking Fees

_ _ _ _ _ Insurance

_ _ _ _ _ Public Transport

Entertainment

_ _ _ _ _ Movies

_ _ _ _ _ Concerts/Events

_ _ _ _ _ Hobbies

_ _ _ _ _ Restaurants

_ _ _ _ _ Parties

_ _ _ _ _ Leisure Travel

Shopping

_ _ _ _ _ Clothes

_ _ _ _ _ Electronics

_ _ _ _ _ Beauty

_ _ _ _ _ Home Goods

_ _ _ _ _ Gifts

Medical

_ _ _ _ _ Doctor Visits

_ _ _ _ _ Medications

_ _ _ _ _ Health Insurance

Fitness

_ _ _ _ _ Gym Memberships

_ _ _ _ _ Sports Equipment

_ _ _ _ _ Wellness Products

Family & Education

_ _ _ _ _ Childcare

_ _ _ _ _ Tuition Fees

_ _ _ _ _ Books

_ _ _ _ _ Materials

_ _ _ _ _ Courses

Month 21

Vision and Transition Goals

_____
_____
_____
_____
_____
_____
_____
_____
_____
_____
_____
_____
_____
_____
_____
_____
_____
_____
_____
_____
_____
_____

Identify Benefits

Evaluate Finances

_____

_____

_____

_____

_____

_____

_____

_____

_____

_____

_____

_____

_____

_____

_____

_____

_____

_____

_____

_____

Skills and
Career Assessment

Preliminary Transition Budget

_____

_____

_____

_____

_____

_____

_____

_____

_____

_____

_____

_____

_____

_____

_____

_____

_____

Notes

Estimated Budget
21 Months Prior to Transition

Fixed Expenses

_ _ _ _ _ Rent/Mortgage

_ _ _ _ _ Electricity

_ _ _ _ _ Water

_ _ _ _ _ Gas

_ _ _ _ _ Internet

_ _ _ _ _ Phone

Food

_ _ _ _ _ Groceries

_ _ _ _ _ Coffee

_ _ _ _ _ Snacks

Transportation

_ _ _ _ _ Fuel

_ _ _ _ _ Maintenance

_ _ _ _ _ Parking Fees

_ _ _ _ _ Insurance

_ _ _ _ _ Public Transport

Entertainment

_ _ _ _ _ Movies

_ _ _ _ _ Concerts/Events

_ _ _ _ _ Hobbies

_ _ _ _ _ Restaurants

_ _ _ _ _ Parties

_ _ _ _ _ Leisure Travel

Shopping

_ _ _ _ _ Clothes

_ _ _ _ _ Electronics

_ _ _ _ _ Beauty

_ _ _ _ _ Home Goods

_ _ _ _ _ Gifts

Medical

_ _ _ _ _ Doctor Visits

_ _ _ _ _ Medications

_ _ _ _ _ Health Insurance

Fitness

_ _ _ _ _ Gym Memberships

_ _ _ _ _ Sports Equipment

_ _ _ _ _ Wellness Products

Family & Education

_ _ _ _ _ Childcare

_ _ _ _ _ Tuition Fees

_ _ _ _ _ Books

_ _ _ _ _ Materials

_ _ _ _ _ Courses

Month 20

Vision and
Transition Goals

_____

_____

_____

_____

_____

_____

_____

_____

_____

_____

_____

_____

_____

_____

_____

_____

_____

_____

_____

_____

Identify Benefits

Evaluate Finances

_____

_____

_____

_____

_____

_____

_____

_____

_____

_____

_____

_____

_____

_____

_____

_____

_____

_____

Skills and
Career Assessment

Preliminary
Transition Budget

Notes

Estimated Budget
20 Months Prior to Transition

Fixed Expenses

_____ Rent/Mortgage

_____ Electricity

_____ Water

_____ Gas

_____ Internet

_____ Phone

Food

_____ Groceries

_____ Coffee

_____ Snacks

Transportation

_____ Fuel

_____ Maintenance

_____ Parking Fees

_____ Insurance

_____ Public Transport

Entertainment

_____ Movies

_____ Concerts/Events

_____ Hobbies

_____ Restaurants

_____ Parties

_____ Leisure Travel

Shopping

_____ Clothes

_____ Electronics

_____ Beauty

_____ Home Goods

_____ Gifts

Medical

_____ Doctor Visits

_____ Medications

_____ Health Insurance

Fitness

_____ Gym Memberships

_____ Sports Equipment

_____ Wellness Products

Family & Education

_____ Childcare

_____ Tuition Fees

_____ Books

_____ Materials

_____ Courses

Month 19

Vision and
Transition Goals

_____

_____

_____

_____

_____

_____

_____

_____

_____

_____

_____

_____

_____

_____

_____

_____

_____

_____

_____

Identify Benefits

Evaluate Finances

_____

_____

_____

_____

_____

_____

_____

_____

_____

_____

_____

_____

_____

_____

_____

_____

_____

_____

Skills and
Career Assessment

Preliminary
Transition Budget

_____
_____
_____
_____
_____
_____
_____
_____
_____
_____
_____
_____
_____
_____
_____
_____
_____
_____
_____
_____

Notes

Estimated Budget
19 Months Prior to Transition

Fixed Expenses

_ _ _ _ _ Rent/Mortgage

_ _ _ _ _ Electricity

_ _ _ _ _ Water

_ _ _ _ _ Gas

_ _ _ _ _ Internet

_ _ _ _ _ Phone

Food

_ _ _ _ _ Groceries

_ _ _ _ _ Coffee

_ _ _ _ _ Snacks

Transportation

_ _ _ _ _ Fuel

_ _ _ _ _ Maintenance

_ _ _ _ _ Parking Fees

_ _ _ _ _ Insurance

_ _ _ _ _ Public Transport

Entertainment

_ _ _ _ _ Movies

_ _ _ _ _ Concerts/Events

_ _ _ _ _ Hobbies

_ _ _ _ _ Restaurants

_ _ _ _ _ Parties

_ _ _ _ _ Leisure Travel

Shopping

_ _ _ _ _ Clothes

_ _ _ _ _ Electronics

_ _ _ _ _ Beauty

_ _ _ _ _ Home Goods

_ _ _ _ _ Gifts

Medical

_ _ _ _ _ Doctor Visits

_ _ _ _ _ Medications

_ _ _ _ _ Health Insurance

Fitness

_ _ _ _ _ Gym Memberships

_ _ _ _ _ Sports Equipment

_ _ _ _ _ Wellness Products

Family & Education

_ _ _ _ _ Childcare

_ _ _ _ _ Tuition Fees

_ _ _ _ _ Books

_ _ _ _ _ Materials

_ _ _ _ _ Courses

Month 18

Vision and
Transition Goals

_____
_____
_____
_____
_____
_____
_____
_____
_____
_____
_____
_____
_____
_____
_____
_____
_____
_____
_____
_____
_____

Identify Benefits

Evaluate Finances

_____

_____

_____

_____

_____

_____

_____

_____

_____

_____

_____

_____

_____

_____

_____

_____

_____

_____

_____

Skills and
Career Assessment

Preliminary Transition Budget

Notes

Estimated Budget
18 Months Prior to Transition

Fixed Expenses

_ _ _ _ _ Rent/Mortgage

_ _ _ _ _ Electricity

_ _ _ _ _ Water

_ _ _ _ _ Gas

_ _ _ _ _ Internet

_ _ _ _ _ Phone

Food

_ _ _ _ _ Groceries

_ _ _ _ _ Coffee

_ _ _ _ _ Snacks

Transportation

_ _ _ _ _ Fuel

_ _ _ _ _ Maintenance

_ _ _ _ _ Parking Fees

_ _ _ _ _ Insurance

_ _ _ _ _ Public Transport

Entertainment

_ _ _ _ _ Movies

_ _ _ _ _ Concerts/Events

_ _ _ _ _ Hobbies

_ _ _ _ _ Restaurants

_ _ _ _ _ Parties

_ _ _ _ _ Leisure Travel

Shopping

_ _ _ _ _ Clothes

_ _ _ _ _ Electronics

_ _ _ _ _ Beauty

_ _ _ _ _ Home Goods

_ _ _ _ _ Gifts

Medical

_ _ _ _ _ Doctor Visits

_ _ _ _ _ Medications

_ _ _ _ _ Health Insurance

Fitness

_ _ _ _ _ Gym Memberships

_ _ _ _ _ Sports Equipment

_ _ _ _ _ Wellness Products

Family & Education

_ _ _ _ _ Childcare

_ _ _ _ _ Tuition Fees

_ _ _ _ _ Books

_ _ _ _ _ Materials

_ _ _ _ _ Courses

Phase 2
17 - 12 Months Prior
to Transition

Creating Stability

Phase 2
17 – 12 Months Prior To Transition
Creating Stability

Phase 2 is about creating stability in the early phases of your transition planning to ensure a smooth transition. Building financial stability through budgeting, saving, and managing debt reduces stress and prepares you for a sustainable lifestyle.

If your desire is to seek civilian employment, career planning and networking helps to ensure you are ready to enter civilian life with confidence. Preparing for healthcare needs and family adjustments will provide a peace of mind. Establishing stability during this phase sets the groundwork for a secure, balanced, and fulfilling transition.

As you prepare for transition, here are a few specific things to consider 18 – 12 months prior:

- **Family Readiness:** Review transition plans with your family to prepare for lifestyle changes.

- **Debt Management:** List all remaining debt and develop a plan for repayment, especially high-interest debts.

Phase 2
17 - 12 Months Prior To Transition
Creating Stability
cont.

- **Savings and Investments:** Add more to your savings and investment transition accounts, if possible and consider other investment options for long-term progress.

- **Career and Networking:** Update your resume, attend informational interviews and seminars and build your civilian network.

- **Healthcare:** Compare civilian healthcare plans and factor estimated costs into your transition budget.

Stability begins with preparation. Focus on building your network, managing your finances, and involving your support system early in the process.

Month 17

Family Readiness

Debt Management

Savings and Investments

Career and Networking

Healthcare

_____

_____

_____

_____

_____

_____

_____

_____

_____

_____

_____

_____

_____

_____

_____

_____

Notes

Estimated Budget
17 Months Prior to Transition

Fixed Expenses

_____Rent/Mortgage

_____Electricity

_____Water

_____Gas

_____Internet

_____Phone

Food

_____Groceries

_____Coffee

_____Snacks

Transportation

_____Fuel

_____Maintenance

_____Parking Fees

_____Insurance

_____Public Transport

Entertainment

_____Movies

_____Concerts/Events

_____Hobbies

_____Restaurants

_____Parties

_____Leisure Travel

Shopping

_____Clothes

_____Electronics

_____Beauty

_____Home Goods

_____Gifts

Medical

_____Doctor Visits

_____Medications

_____Health Insurance

Fitness

_____Gym Memberships

_____Sports Equipment

_____Wellness Products

Family & Education

_____Childcare

_____Tuition Fees

_____Books

_____Materials

_____Courses

Month 16

Family Readiness

Debt Management

_____

_____

_____

_____

_____

_____

_____

_____

_____

_____

_____

_____

_____

_____

_____

_____

_____

_____

Savings and Investments

Career and Networking

Healthcare

Notes

Estimated Budget
16 Months Prior to Transition

Fixed Expenses

_____Rent/Mortgage

_____Electricity

_____Water

_____Gas

_____Internet

_____Phone

Food

_____Groceries

_____Coffee

_____Snacks

Transportation

_____Fuel

_____Maintenance

_____Parking Fees

_____Insurance

_____Public Transport

Entertainment

_____Movies

_____Concerts/Events

_____Hobbies

_____Restaurants

_____Parties

_____Leisure Travel

Shopping

_____Clothes

_____Electronics

_____Beauty

_____Home Goods

_____Gifts

Medical

_____Doctor Visits

_____Medications

_____Health Insurance

Fitness

_____Gym Memberships

_____Sports Equipment

_____Wellness Products

Family & Education

_____Childcare

_____Tuition Fees

_____Books

_____Materials

_____Courses

94

Month 15

Family Readiness

Debt Management

Savings and Investments

Career and Networking

Healthcare

Notes

Estimated Budget
15 Months Prior to Transition

Fixed Expenses

_ _ _ _ _Rent/Mortgage

_ _ _ _ _Electricity

_ _ _ _ _Water

_ _ _ _ _Gas

_ _ _ _ _Internet

_ _ _ _ _Phone

Food

_ _ _ _ _Groceries

_ _ _ _ _Coffee

_ _ _ _ _Snacks

Transportation

_ _ _ _ _Fuel

_ _ _ _ _Maintenance

_ _ _ _ _Parking Fees

_ _ _ _ _Insurance

_ _ _ _ _Public Transport

Entertainment

_ _ _ _ _Movies

_ _ _ _ _Concerts/Events

_ _ _ _ _Hobbies

_ _ _ _ _Restaurants

_ _ _ _ _Parties

_ _ _ _ _Leisure Travel

Shopping

_ _ _ _ _Clothes

_ _ _ _ _Electronics

_ _ _ _ _Beauty

_ _ _ _ _Home Goods

_ _ _ _ _Gifts

Medical

_ _ _ _ _Doctor Visits

_ _ _ _ _Medications

_ _ _ _ _Health Insurance

Fitness

_ _ _ _ _Gym Memberships

_ _ _ _ _Sports Equipment

_ _ _ _ _Wellness Products

Family & Education

_ _ _ _ _Childcare

_ _ _ _ _Tuition Fees

_ _ _ _ _Books

_ _ _ _ _Materials

_ _ _ _ _Courses

Month 14

Family Readiness

Debt Management

Savings and Investments

Career and Networking

Healthcare

Notes

Estimated Budget
14 Months Prior to Transition

Fixed Expenses

_ _ _ _ _ Rent/Mortgage

_ _ _ _ _ Electricity

_ _ _ _ _ Water

_ _ _ _ _ Gas

_ _ _ _ _ Internet

_ _ _ _ _ Phone

Food

_ _ _ _ _ Groceries

_ _ _ _ _ Coffee

_ _ _ _ _ Snacks

Transportation

_ _ _ _ _ Fuel

_ _ _ _ _ Maintenance

_ _ _ _ _ Parking Fees

_ _ _ _ _ Insurance

_ _ _ _ _ Public Transport

Entertainment

_ _ _ _ _ Movies

_ _ _ _ _ Concerts/Events

_ _ _ _ _ Hobbies

_ _ _ _ _ Restaurants

_ _ _ _ _ Parties

_ _ _ _ _ Leisure Travel

Shopping

_ _ _ _ _ Clothes

_ _ _ _ _ Electronics

_ _ _ _ _ Beauty

_ _ _ _ _ Home Goods

_ _ _ _ _ Gifts

Medical

_ _ _ _ _ Doctor Visits

_ _ _ _ _ Medications

_ _ _ _ _ Health Insurance

Fitness

_ _ _ _ _ Gym Memberships

_ _ _ _ _ Sports Equipment

_ _ _ _ _ Wellness Products

Family & Education

_ _ _ _ _ Childcare

_ _ _ _ _ Tuition Fees

_ _ _ _ _ Books

_ _ _ _ _ Materials

_ _ _ _ _ Courses

Month 13

Family Readiness

Debt Management

Savings and Investments

Career and Networking

Healthcare

Notes

Estimated Budget
13 Months Prior to Transition

Fixed Expenses

_ _ _ _ _ Rent/Mortgage

_ _ _ _ _ Electricity

_ _ _ _ _ Water

_ _ _ _ _ Gas

_ _ _ _ _ Internet

_ _ _ _ _ Phone

Food

_ _ _ _ _ Groceries

_ _ _ _ _ Coffee

_ _ _ _ _ Snacks

Transportation

_ _ _ _ _ Fuel

_ _ _ _ _ Maintenance

_ _ _ _ _ Parking Fees

_ _ _ _ _ Insurance

_ _ _ _ _ Public Transport

Entertainment

_ _ _ _ _ Movies

_ _ _ _ _ Concerts/Events

_ _ _ _ _ Hobbies

_ _ _ _ _ Restaurants

_ _ _ _ _ Parties

_ _ _ _ _ Leisure Travel

Shopping

_ _ _ _ _ Clothes

_ _ _ _ _ Electronics

_ _ _ _ _ Beauty

_ _ _ _ _ Home Goods

_ _ _ _ _ Gifts

Medical

_ _ _ _ _ Doctor Visits

_ _ _ _ _ Medications

_ _ _ _ _ Health Insurance

Fitness

_ _ _ _ _ Gym Memberships

_ _ _ _ _ Sports Equipment

_ _ _ _ _ Wellness Products

Family & Education

_ _ _ _ _ Childcare

_ _ _ _ _ Tuition Fees

_ _ _ _ _ Books

_ _ _ _ _ Materials

_ _ _ _ _ Courses

Month 12

Family Readiness

Debt Management

Savings and Investments

Career and Networking

Healthcare

Notes

Estimated Budget
12 Months Prior to Transition

Fixed Expenses

_ _ _ _ _ Rent/Mortgage

_ _ _ _ _ Electricity

_ _ _ _ _ Water

_ _ _ _ _ Gas

_ _ _ _ _ Internet

_ _ _ _ _ Phone

Food

_ _ _ _ _ Groceries

_ _ _ _ _ Coffee

_ _ _ _ _ Snacks

Transportation

_ _ _ _ _ Fuel

_ _ _ _ _ Maintenance

_ _ _ _ _ Parking Fees

_ _ _ _ _ Insurance

_ _ _ _ _ Public Transport

Entertainment

_ _ _ _ _ Movies

_ _ _ _ _ Concerts/Events

_ _ _ _ _ Hobbies

_ _ _ _ _ Restaurants

_ _ _ _ _ Parties

_ _ _ _ _ Leisure Travel

Shopping

_ _ _ _ _ Clothes

_ _ _ _ _ Electronics

_ _ _ _ _ Beauty

_ _ _ _ _ Home Goods

_ _ _ _ _ Gifts

Medical

_ _ _ _ _ Doctor Visits

_ _ _ _ _ Medications

_ _ _ _ _ Health Insurance

Fitness

_ _ _ _ _ Gym Memberships

_ _ _ _ _ Sports Equipment

_ _ _ _ _ Wellness Products

Family & Education

_ _ _ _ _ Childcare

_ _ _ _ _ Tuition Fees

_ _ _ _ _ Books

_ _ _ _ _ Materials

_ _ _ _ _ Courses

126

<u>Phase 3</u>
11 – 6 Months
Prior to Transition

Putting Your
Plans Into Action

Phase 3
11 – 6 Months Prior To Transition
Putting Your Plans Into Action

Phase 3 is about putting your plans into action. This is the time to consider job applications, healthcare decisions, and budget adjustments with realistic post-transition costs. Putting your plans into action during this phase helps ensure a smooth, confident transition into civilian life, with everything set in place for your next chapter.

As you prepare for transition, here are a few specific things to consider 11 – 6 months prior:

- **Job Applications and Interview Preparations:** Enthusiastically start applying for jobs, conduct mock interviews, and review negotiation strategies for civilian employment.

- **Benefits and VA Enrollment:** Submit VA benefits applications and gather necessary documentation for a smooth transition.

- **Revisit Your Financial Plan:** Revise your budget with actual costs for housing, transportation, and other transition expenses.

Phase 3

11 – 6 Months Prior To Transition
Putting Your Plans Into Action
cont.

- **Relocation and Housing:** Research your housing options and budget for relocation, if applicable.

- **Banking:** Open a civilian bank account if needed.

- **Insurance:** Consider the types of insurance that you and your family may need.

Now is the time for you to take action. Stay organized and focused—tackle one task at a time to reduce stress and keep your transition on track.

Month 11

Job Applications and Interview Preparations

Benefits and VA Enrollment

Revisit Your
Financial Plan

Banking

Insurance

Notes

Estimated Budget
11 Months Prior to Transition

Fixed Expenses

_ _ _ _ _ Rent/Mortgage

_ _ _ _ _ Electricity

_ _ _ _ _ Water

_ _ _ _ _ Gas

_ _ _ _ _ Internet

_ _ _ _ _ Phone

Food

_ _ _ _ _ Groceries

_ _ _ _ _ Coffee

_ _ _ _ _ Snacks

Transportation

_ _ _ _ _ Fuel

_ _ _ _ _ Maintenance

_ _ _ _ _ Parking Fees

_ _ _ _ _ Insurance

_ _ _ _ _ Public Transport

Entertainment

_ _ _ _ _ Movies

_ _ _ _ _ Concerts/Events

_ _ _ _ _ Hobbies

_ _ _ _ _ Restaurants

_ _ _ _ _ Parties

_ _ _ _ _ Leisure Travel

Shopping

_ _ _ _ _ Clothes

_ _ _ _ _ Electronics

_ _ _ _ _ Beauty

_ _ _ _ _ Home Goods

_ _ _ _ _ Gifts

Medical

_ _ _ _ _ Doctor Visits

_ _ _ _ _ Medications

_ _ _ _ _ Health Insurance

Fitness

_ _ _ _ _ Gym Memberships

_ _ _ _ _ Sports Equipment

_ _ _ _ _ Wellness Products

Family & Education

_ _ _ _ _ Childcare

_ _ _ _ _ Tuition Fees

_ _ _ _ _ Books

_ _ _ _ _ Materials

_ _ _ _ _ Courses

Month 10

Job Applications and Interview Preparations

_____

_____

_____

_____

_____

_____

_____

_____

_____

_____

_____

_____

_____

_____

_____

_____

_____

_____

_____

_____

_____

Benefits and
VA Enrollment

Revisit Your
Financial Plan

_____

_____

_____

_____

_____

_____

_____

_____

_____

_____

_____

_____

_____

_____

_____

_____

_____

_____

Banking

Insurance

_____
_____
_____
_____
_____
_____
_____
_____
_____
_____
_____
_____
_____
_____
_____
_____
_____
_____
_____

Notes

Estimated Budget
10 Months Prior to Transition

Fixed Expenses

_____Rent/Mortgage

_____Electricity

_____Water

_____Gas

_____Internet

_____Phone

Food

_____Groceries

_____Coffee

_____Snacks

Transportation

_____Fuel

_____Maintenance

_____Parking Fees

_____Insurance

_____Public Transport

Entertainment

_____Movies

_____Concerts/Events

_____Hobbies

_____Restaurants

_____Parties

_____Leisure Travel

Shopping

_____Clothes

_____Electronics

_____Beauty

_____Home Goods

_____Gifts

Medical

_____Doctor Visits

_____Medications

_____Health Insurance

Fitness

_____Gym Memberships

_____Sports Equipment

_____Wellness Products

Family & Education

_____Childcare

_____Tuition Fees

_____Books

_____Materials

_____Courses

Month 9

Job Applications and Interview Preparations

Benefits and VA Enrollment

Revisit Your Financial Plan

Banking

Insurance

Notes

Estimated Budget
9 Months Prior to Transition

Fixed Expenses

_ _ _ _ _ Rent/Mortgage

_ _ _ _ _ Electricity

_ _ _ _ _ Water

_ _ _ _ _ Gas

_ _ _ _ _ Internet

_ _ _ _ _ Phone

Food

_ _ _ _ _ Groceries

_ _ _ _ _ Coffee

_ _ _ _ _ Snacks

Transportation

_ _ _ _ _ Fuel

_ _ _ _ _ Maintenance

_ _ _ _ _ Parking Fees

_ _ _ _ _ Insurance

_ _ _ _ _ Public Transport

Entertainment

_ _ _ _ _ Movies

_ _ _ _ _ Concerts/Events

_ _ _ _ _ Hobbies

_ _ _ _ _ Restaurants

_ _ _ _ _ Parties

_ _ _ _ _ Leisure Travel

Shopping

_ _ _ _ _ Clothes

_ _ _ _ _ Electronics

_ _ _ _ _ Beauty

_ _ _ _ _ Home Goods

_ _ _ _ _ Gifts

Medical

_ _ _ _ _ Doctor Visits

_ _ _ _ _ Medications

_ _ _ _ _ Health Insurance

Fitness

_ _ _ _ _ Gym Memberships

_ _ _ _ _ Sports Equipment

_ _ _ _ _ Wellness Products

Family & Education

_ _ _ _ _ Childcare

_ _ _ _ _ Tuition Fees

_ _ _ _ _ Books

_ _ _ _ _ Materials

_ _ _ _ _ Courses

Month 8

Job Applications and Interview Preparations

Benefits and
VA Enrollment

Revisit Your
Financial Plan

Banking

Insurance

Notes

Estimated Budget
8 Months Prior to Transition

Fixed Expenses

_ _ _ _ _ Rent/Mortgage

_ _ _ _ _ Electricity

_ _ _ _ _ Water

_ _ _ _ _ Gas

_ _ _ _ _ Internet

_ _ _ _ _ Phone

Food

_ _ _ _ _ Groceries

_ _ _ _ _ Coffee

_ _ _ _ _ Snacks

Transportation

_ _ _ _ _ Fuel

_ _ _ _ _ Maintenance

_ _ _ _ _ Parking Fees

_ _ _ _ _ Insurance

_ _ _ _ _ Public Transport

Entertainment

_ _ _ _ _ Movies

_ _ _ _ _ Concerts/Events

_ _ _ _ _ Hobbies

_ _ _ _ _ Restaurants

_ _ _ _ _ Parties

_ _ _ _ _ Leisure Travel

Shopping

_ _ _ _ _ Clothes

_ _ _ _ _ Electronics

_ _ _ _ _ Beauty

_ _ _ _ _ Home Goods

_ _ _ _ _ Gifts

Medical

_ _ _ _ _ Doctor Visits

_ _ _ _ _ Medications

_ _ _ _ _ Health Insurance

Fitness

_ _ _ _ _ Gym Memberships

_ _ _ _ _ Sports Equipment

_ _ _ _ _ Wellness Products

Family & Education

_ _ _ _ _ Childcare

_ _ _ _ _ Tuition Fees

_ _ _ _ _ Books

_ _ _ _ _ Materials

_ _ _ _ _ Courses

Month 7

Job Applications and Interview Preparations

Benefits and
VA Enrollment

Revisit Your
Financial Plan

Banking

Insurance

_____

_____

_____

_____

_____

_____

_____

_____

_____

_____

_____

_____

_____

_____

_____

_____

_____

_____

_____

Notes

Estimated Budget
7 Months Prior to Transition

Fixed Expenses

_ _ _ _ _Rent/Mortgage

_ _ _ _ _Electricity

_ _ _ _ _Water

_ _ _ _ _Gas

_ _ _ _ _Internet

_ _ _ _ _Phone

Food

_ _ _ _ _Groceries

_ _ _ _ _Coffee

_ _ _ _ _Snacks

Transportation

_ _ _ _ _Fuel

_ _ _ _ _Maintenance

_ _ _ _ _Parking Fees

_ _ _ _ _Insurance

_ _ _ _ _Public Transport

Entertainment

_ _ _ _ _Movies

_ _ _ _ _Concerts/Events

_ _ _ _ _Hobbies

_ _ _ _ _Restaurants

_ _ _ _ _Parties

_ _ _ _ _Leisure Travel

Shopping

_ _ _ _ _Clothes

_ _ _ _ _Electronics

_ _ _ _ _Beauty

_ _ _ _ _Home Goods

_ _ _ _ _Gifts

Medical

_ _ _ _ _Doctor Visits

_ _ _ _ _Medications

_ _ _ _ _Health Insurance

Fitness

_ _ _ _ _Gym Memberships

_ _ _ _ _Sports Equipment

_ _ _ _ _Wellness Products

Family & Education

_ _ _ _ _Childcare

_ _ _ _ _Tuition Fees

_ _ _ _ _Books

_ _ _ _ _Materials

_ _ _ _ _Courses

Month 6

Job Applications and Interview Preparations

Benefits and
VA Enrollment

Revisit Your Financial Plan

_____
_____
_____
_____
_____
_____
_____
_____
_____
_____
_____
_____
_____
_____
_____
_____
_____
_____

Banking

Insurance

_____

_____

_____

_____

_____

_____

_____

_____

_____

_____

_____

_____

_____

_____

_____

_____

_____

_____

_____

_____

_____

Notes

Estimated Budget
6 Months Prior to Transition

Fixed Expenses

_ _ _ _ _Rent/Mortgage

_ _ _ _ _Electricity

_ _ _ _ _Water

_ _ _ _ _Gas

_ _ _ _Internet

_ _ _ _ _Phone

Food

_ _ _ _ _Groceries

_ _ _ _ _Coffee

_ _ _ _ _Snacks

Transportation

_ _ _ _ _Fuel

_ _ _ _ _Maintenance

_ _ _ _ _Parking Fees

_ _ _ _ _Insurance

_ _ _ _ _Public Transport

Entertainment

_ _ _ _ _Movies

_ _ _ _ _Concerts/Events

_ _ _ _ _Hobbies

_ _ _ _ _Restaurants

_ _ _ _ _Parties

_ _ _ _ _Leisure Travel

Shopping

_ _ _ _ _Clothes

_ _ _ _ _Electronics

_ _ _ _ _Beauty

_ _ _ _ _Home Goods

_ _ _ _ _Gifts

Medical

_ _ _ _ _Doctor Visits

_ _ _ _ _Medications

_ _ _ _ _Health Insurance

Fitness

_ _ _ _ _Gym Memberships

_ _ _ _ _Sports Equipment

_ _ _ _ _Wellness Products

Family & Education

_ _ _ _ _Childcare

_ _ _ _ _Tuition Fees

_ _ _ _ _Books

_ _ _ _ _Materials

_ _ _ _ _Courses

Phase 4

5 – 3 Months
Prior to Transition

Finalizing Your
Transition Plans

Phase 4
5 - 3 Months Prior To Transition
Finalizing Your Transition Plans

Phase 4 is all about finalizing your transition plans. Confirm that your transition income, benefits, and healthcare benefits are ready. Ensure your family is prepared for any changes. This is also the time for any medical checkups and wellness planning. These steps throughout this phase will help to ensure you are fully equipped and ready for a successful transition.

As you prepare for transition, here are a few specific things to consider 5 - 3 months prior:

- **Verify Transition Income and Benefits:** Verify that all pension payments, healthcare benefits, and VA benefits are set up and ready to go.

- **Transition Preparation for Family Members:** Prepare family for new routines and adjustments.

- **Medical and Dental Checkups:** Complete medical and dental checkups before final transition.

- **Emergency Fund Verification:** Make sure your emergency fund can cover at least 3-6 months of living expenses and essential financial obligations.

Quick Tip:

Double-check your separation plans and benefits. Taking a few extra minutes now can save you hours of frustration and unexpected setbacks later.

Month 5

Verify Transition Income and Benefits

_____

_____

_____

_____

_____

_____

_____

_____

_____

_____

_____

_____

_____

_____

_____

_____

_____

Transition Preparation for Family Members

Medical and Dental Checkups

Emergency
Fund Verification

Notes

Estimated Budget
5 Months Prior to Transition

Fixed Expenses

_ _ _ _ _ Rent/Mortgage

_ _ _ _ _ Electricity

_ _ _ _ _ Water

_ _ _ _ _ Gas

_ _ _ _ _ Internet

_ _ _ _ _ Phone

Food

_ _ _ _ _ Groceries

_ _ _ _ _ Coffee

_ _ _ _ _ Snacks

Transportation

_ _ _ _ _ Fuel

_ _ _ _ _ Maintenance

_ _ _ _ _ Parking Fees

_ _ _ _ _ Insurance

_ _ _ _ _ Public Transport

Entertainment

_ _ _ _ _ Movies

_ _ _ _ _ Concerts/Events

_ _ _ _ _ Hobbies

_ _ _ _ _ Restaurants

_ _ _ _ _ Parties

_ _ _ _ _ Leisure Travel

Shopping

_ _ _ _ _ Clothes

_ _ _ _ _ Electronics

_ _ _ _ _ Beauty

_ _ _ _ _ Home Goods

_ _ _ _ _ Gifts

Medical

_ _ _ _ _ Doctor Visits

_ _ _ _ _ Medications

_ _ _ _ _ Health Insurance

Fitness

_ _ _ _ _ Gym Memberships

_ _ _ _ _ Sports Equipment

_ _ _ _ _ Wellness Products

Family & Education

_ _ _ _ _ Childcare

_ _ _ _ _ Tuition Fees

_ _ _ _ _ Books

_ _ _ _ _ Materials

_ _ _ _ _ Courses

Month 4

Verify Transition Income and Benefits

Transition Preparation for Family Members

Medical and
Dental Checkups

Emergency Fund Verification

Notes

Estimated Budget
4 Months Prior to Transition

Fixed Expenses

_ _ _ _ _ Rent/Mortgage

_ _ _ _ _ Electricity

_ _ _ _ _ Water

_ _ _ _ _ Gas

_ _ _ _ _ Internet

_ _ _ _ _ Phone

Food

_ _ _ _ _ Groceries

_ _ _ _ _ Coffee

_ _ _ _ _ Snacks

Transportation

_ _ _ _ _ Fuel

_ _ _ _ _ Maintenance

_ _ _ _ _ Parking Fees

_ _ _ _ _ Insurance

_ _ _ _ _ Public Transport

Entertainment

_ _ _ _ _ Movies

_ _ _ _ _ Concerts/Events

_ _ _ _ _ Hobbies

_ _ _ _ _ Restaurants

_ _ _ _ _ Parties

_ _ _ _ _ Leisure Travel

Shopping

_ _ _ _ _ Clothes

_ _ _ _ _ Electronics

_ _ _ _ _ Beauty

_ _ _ _ _ Home Goods

_ _ _ _ _ Gifts

Medical

_ _ _ _ _ Doctor Visits

_ _ _ _ _ Medications

_ _ _ _ _ Health Insurance

Fitness

_ _ _ _ _ Gym Memberships

_ _ _ _ _ Sports Equipment

_ _ _ _ _ Wellness Products

Family & Education

_ _ _ _ _ Childcare

_ _ _ _ _ Tuition Fees

_ _ _ _ _ Books

_ _ _ _ _ Materials

_ _ _ _ _ Courses

Month 3

Verify Transition Income and Benefits

Transition Preparation for Family Members

Medical and
Dental Checkups

Emergency
Fund Verification

Notes

Estimated Budget
3 Months Prior to Transition

Fixed Expenses

_ _ _ _ _Rent/Mortgage

_ _ _ _ _Electricity

_ _ _ _ _Water

_ _ _ _ _Gas

_ _ _ _ _Internet

_ _ _ _ _Phone

Food

_ _ _ _ _Groceries

_ _ _ _ _Coffee

_ _ _ _ _Snacks

Transportation

_ _ _ _ _Fuel

_ _ _ _ _Maintenance

_ _ _ _ _Parking Fees

_ _ _ _ _Insurance

_ _ _ _ _Public Transport

Entertainment

_ _ _ _ _Movies

_ _ _ _ _Concerts/Events

_ _ _ _ _Hobbies

_ _ _ _ _Restaurants

_ _ _ _ _Parties

_ _ _ _ _Leisure Travel

Shopping

_ _ _ _ _Clothes

_ _ _ _ _Electronics

_ _ _ _ _Beauty

_ _ _ _ _Home Goods

_ _ _ _ _Gifts

Medical

_ _ _ _ _Doctor Visits

_ _ _ _ _Medications

_ _ _ _ _Health Insurance

Fitness

_ _ _ _ _Gym Memberships

_ _ _ _ _Sports Equipment

_ _ _ _ _Wellness Products

Family & Education

_ _ _ _ _Childcare

_ _ _ _ _Tuition Fees

_ _ _ _ _Books

_ _ _ _ _Materials

_ _ _ _ _Courses

Phase 5
2 – 0 Months
Prior to Transition

Your Separation

Phase 5
2 – 0 Months Prior To Transition
Your Separation

Phase 5 focuses on final preparations for separation while reflecting on your unique journey. Complete any remaining paperwork to ensure a smooth transition. Establish new routines and take time to set personal goals for your next chapter. Reflect on all of your past accomplishments and look forward to what's ahead in your future. These final steps will help your transition to civilian life with purpose and confidence.

As you prepare for transition, here are a few specific things to consider 2 - 0 months prior:

- **Finalize Your Transition Paperwork:** Confirm all military exit requirements, including final pay, leave balances, and last-minute tasks.

- **Establish New Routines:** Establish new routines, support systems, and goals for your transition.

- **Reflection and Celebration:** Consider hosting a thoughtful gathering to honor your service and mark the transition, while mentally preparing for the next chapter in your journey.

Pause to reflect on your service experience, and set small, achievable goals to guide your first steps into civilian life.

Month 2

Finalize
Transition Paperwork

Establish New Routine

Reflection and Celebration

Notes

Estimated Budget
2 Months Prior to Transition

Fixed Expenses

_ _ _ _ _ Rent/Mortgage

_ _ _ _ _ Electricity

_ _ _ _ _ Water

_ _ _ _ _ Gas

_ _ _ _ _ Internet

_ _ _ _ _ Phone

Food

_ _ _ _ _ Groceries

_ _ _ _ _ Coffee

_ _ _ _ _ Snacks

Transportation

_ _ _ _ _ Fuel

_ _ _ _ _ Maintenance

_ _ _ _ _ Parking Fees

_ _ _ _ _ Insurance

_ _ _ _ _ Public Transport

Entertainment

_ _ _ _ _ Movies

_ _ _ _ _ Concerts/Events

_ _ _ _ _ Hobbies

_ _ _ _ _ Restaurants

_ _ _ _ _ Parties

_ _ _ _ _ Leisure Travel

Shopping

_ _ _ _ _ Clothes

_ _ _ _ _ Electronics

_ _ _ _ _ Beauty

_ _ _ _ _ Home Goods

_ _ _ _ _ Gifts

Medical

_ _ _ _ _ Doctor Visits

_ _ _ _ _ Medications

_ _ _ _ _ Health Insurance

Fitness

_ _ _ _ _ Gym Memberships

_ _ _ _ _ Sports Equipment

_ _ _ _ _ Wellness Products

Family & Education

_ _ _ _ _ Childcare

_ _ _ _ _ Tuition Fees

_ _ _ _ _ Books

_ _ _ _ _ Materials

_ _ _ _ _ Courses

Month 1

Finalize
Transition Paperwork

Establish New Routine

Reflection and Celebration

Notes

Estimated Budget
1 Month Prior to Transition

Fixed Expenses

_____Rent/Mortgage

_____Electricity

_____Water

_____Gas

_____Internet

_____Phone

Food

_____Groceries

_____Coffee

_____Snacks

Transportation

_____Fuel

_____Maintenance

_____Parking Fees

_____Insurance

_____Public Transport

Entertainment

_____Movies

_____Concerts/Events

_____Hobbies

_____Restaurants

_____Parties

_____Leisure Travel

Shopping

_____Clothes

_____Electronics

_____Beauty

_____Home Goods

_____Gifts

Medical

_____Doctor Visits

_____Medications

_____Health Insurance

Fitness

_____Gym Memberships

_____Sports Equipment

_____Wellness Products

Family & Education

_____Childcare

_____Tuition Fees

_____Books

_____Materials

_____Courses

Month o

Finalize
Transition Paperwork

Establish New Routine

Reflection and Celebration

Notes

Estimated Budget
o Month Prior to Transition

Fixed Expenses

_____ Rent/Mortgage

_____ Electricity

_____ Water

_____ Gas

_____ Internet

_____ Phone

Food

_____ Groceries

_____ Coffee

_____ Snacks

Transportation

_____ Fuel

_____ Maintenance

_____ Parking Fees

_____ Insurance

_____ Public Transport

Entertainment

_____ Movies

_____ Concerts/Events

_____ Hobbies

_____ Restaurants

_____ Parties

_____ Leisure Travel

Shopping

_____ Clothes

_____ Electronics

_____ Beauty

_____ Home Goods

_____ Gifts

Medical

_____ Doctor Visits

_____ Medications

_____ Health Insurance

Fitness

_____ Gym Memberships

_____ Sports Equipment

_____ Wellness Products

Family & Education

_____ Childcare

_____ Tuition Fees

_____ Books

_____ Materials

_____ Courses

my personal
Transition
Reflection and
Goal Setting Journaling

my personal
Transition
Reflection and
Goal Setting Journaling

Transition reflection and goal setting is essential in concluding one chapter and beginning your next chapter with intention. After many years of service, taking time to reflect on your military journey allows you to honor your successes, appreciate lessons learned, and acknowledge the resilience you've built along the way. These reflections serve as a basis, helping you to understand how your experiences can shape your path forward.

Journaling within this section allows you to pause and celebrate your proudest moments, as well as to consider the challenges that strengthened you along the way. By reflecting on these experiences, you can gain clarity about the skills, values, and insights you've developed, which will guide your decisions in civilian life.

After you've reflected, shift your focus toward goal-setting for this new phase of your life. Use this journal space to identify personal and professional goals that inspire and motivate you.

Whether it's learning a new skill, starting a business, pursuing hobbies, or engaging in meaningful community work, consider the steps required to accomplish these goals. Break down each step into actionable, manageable tasks to create a clear roadmap for development and success.

Additionally, reassess your financial plans to ensure they align with your new goals and lifestyle. Confirm any necessary budget adjustments based on your transition income, civilian benefits, and other important priorities.

This combination of reflection and intentional goal-setting will help you to move forward with self-confidence, creating a purposeful and fulfilling next chapter.

my personal
Transition
Reflection and
Goal Setting Journaling

my personal
Transition
Reflection and
Goal Setting Journaling

my personal
Transition
Reflection and
Goal Setting Journaling

my personal
Transition
Reflection and
Goal Setting Journaling

my personal
Transition
Reflection and
Goal Setting Journaling

my personal
Transition
Reflection and
Goal Setting Journaling

_____

_____

_____

_____

_____

_____

_____

_____

_____

_____

_____

_____

_____

_____

_____

_____

_____

_____

my personal
Transition
Reflection and
Goal Setting Journaling

my personal
Transition
Reflection and
Goal Setting Journaling

my personal
Transition
Reflection and
Goal Setting Journaling

_____

_____

_____

_____

_____

_____

_____

_____

_____

_____

_____

_____

_____

_____

_____

_____

_____

_____

_____

_____

my personal
**Transition
Reflection and
Goal Setting Journaling**

my personal
Transition
Reflection and
Goal Setting Journaling

my personal
Transition
Reflection and
Goal Setting Journaling

my personal
Transition
Reflection and
Goal Setting Journaling

my personal
Transition
Reflection and
Goal Setting Journaling

my personal
Transition
Reflection and
Goal Setting Journaling

my personal
Transition
Reflection and
Goal Setting Journaling

my personal
Transition
Reflection and
Goal Setting Journaling

my personal

Transition Savings Plan

my personal
Transition Savings Plan

Saving For:		Goal:		

Month	Date	Deposit	Balance	Notes
January				
February				
March				
April				
May				
June				
July				
August				
September				
October				
November				
December				

Saving For:		Goal:		

Month	Date	Deposit	Balance	Notes
January				
February				
March				
April				
May				
June				
July				
August				
September				
October				
November				
December				

my personal
Transition Savings Plan

Saving For:		Goal:		

Month	Date	Deposit	Balance	Notes
January				
February				
March				
April				
May				
June				
July				
August				
September				
October				
November				
December				

Saving For:		Goal:		

Month	Date	Deposit	Balance	Notes
January				
February				
March				
April				
May				
June				
July				
August				
September				
October				
November				
December				

my personal

**Transition Appointment
Reminder and To Do List**

Transition Appointment
Reminder and To Do List

Date	Appointment / To Do's
	☐ _____ ☐ _____ ☐ _____
	☐ _____ ☐ _____ ☐ _____
	☐ _____ ☐ _____ ☐ _____
	☐ _____ ☐ _____ ☐ _____
	☐ _____ ☐ _____ ☐ _____
	☐ _____ ☐ _____ ☐ _____
	☐ _____ ☐ _____ ☐ _____

my personal
Transition Appointment
Reminder and To Do List

Date	Appointment / To Do's

☐ _____
☐ _____
☐ _____

☐ _____
☐ _____
☐ _____

☐ _____
☐ _____
☐ _____

☐ _____
☐ _____
☐ _____

☐ _____
☐ _____
☐ _____

☐ _____
☐ _____
☐ _____

☐ _____
☐ _____
☐ _____

my personal
Transition Appointment
Reminder and To Do List

Date	Appointment / To Do's
	☐ _____ ☐ _____ ☐ _____
	☐ _____ ☐ _____ ☐ _____
	☐ _____ ☐ _____ ☐ _____
	☐ _____ ☐ _____ ☐ _____
	☐ _____ ☐ _____ ☐ _____
	☐ _____ ☐ _____ ☐ _____
	☐ _____ ☐ _____ ☐ _____

Transition Appointment
Reminder and To Do List

Date	Appointment / To Do's
	☐ _____ ☐ _____ ☐ _____
	☐ _____ ☐ _____ ☐ _____
	☐ _____ ☐ _____ ☐ _____
	☐ _____ ☐ _____ ☐ _____
	☐ _____ ☐ _____ ☐ _____
	☐ _____ ☐ _____ ☐ _____
	☐ _____ ☐ _____ ☐ _____

Transition Appointment
Reminder and To Do List

Date	Appointment / To Do's
	☐ _____
	☐ _____
	☐ _____
	☐ _____
	☐ _____
	☐ _____
	☐ _____
	☐ _____
	☐ _____
	☐ _____
	☐ _____
	☐ _____
	☐ _____
	☐ _____
	☐ _____
	☐ _____
	☐ _____
	☐ _____
	☐ _____
	☐ _____
	☐ _____

my personal
Transition Appointment Reminder and To Do List

Date	Appointment / To Do's
	☐ _____ ☐ _____ ☐ _____
	☐ _____ ☐ _____ ☐ _____
	☐ _____ ☐ _____ ☐ _____
	☐ _____ ☐ _____ ☐ _____
	☐ _____ ☐ _____ ☐ _____
	☐ _____ ☐ _____ ☐ _____
	☐ _____ ☐ _____ ☐ _____

my personal
Transition Appointment
Reminder and To Do List

Date	Appointment / To Do's
	☐ _____
	☐ _____
	☐ _____
	☐ _____
	☐ _____
	☐ _____
	☐ _____
	☐ _____
	☐ _____
	☐ _____
	☐ _____
	☐ _____
	☐ _____
	☐ _____
	☐ _____
	☐ _____
	☐ _____
	☐ _____
	☐ _____
	☐ _____
	☐ _____

Transition Appointment
Reminder and To Do List

Date	Appointment / To Do's
	☐ _____ ☐ _____ ☐ _____
	☐ _____ ☐ _____ ☐ _____
	☐ _____ ☐ _____ ☐ _____
	☐ _____ ☐ _____ ☐ _____
	☐ _____ ☐ _____ ☐ _____
	☐ _____ ☐ _____ ☐ _____
	☐ _____ ☐ _____ ☐ _____

Date	Appointment / To Do's
	☐ _____
	☐ _____
	☐ _____
	☐ _____
	☐ _____
	☐ _____
	☐ _____
	☐ _____
	☐ _____
	☐ _____
	☐ _____
	☐ _____
	☐ _____
	☐ _____
	☐ _____
	☐ _____
	☐ _____
	☐ _____
	☐ _____
	☐ _____
	☐ _____

Transition Appointment Reminder and To Do List

Date	Appointment / To Do's
	☐ _____
	☐ _____
	☐ _____
	☐ _____
	☐ _____
	☐ _____
	☐ _____
	☐ _____
	☐ _____
	☐ _____
	☐ _____
	☐ _____
	☐ _____
	☐ _____
	☐ _____
	☐ _____
	☐ _____
	☐ _____
	☐ _____
	☐ _____
	☐ _____

Transition Appointment
Reminder and To Do List

Date	Appointment / To Do's
	☐ _____
	☐ _____
	☐ _____
	☐ _____
	☐ _____
	☐ _____
	☐ _____
	☐ _____
	☐ _____
	☐ _____
	☐ _____
	☐ _____
	☐ _____
	☐ _____
	☐ _____
	☐ _____
	☐ _____
	☐ _____
	☐ _____
	☐ _____
	☐ _____

my personal
Transition Appointment
Reminder and To Do List

Date	Appointment / To Do's
	☐ _____ ☐ _____ ☐ _____
	☐ _____ ☐ _____ ☐ _____
	☐ _____ ☐ _____ ☐ _____
	☐ _____ ☐ _____ ☐ _____
	☐ _____ ☐ _____ ☐ _____
	☐ _____ ☐ _____ ☐ _____
	☐ _____ ☐ _____ ☐ _____

Date	Appointment / To Do's
	☐ _____ ☐ _____ ☐ _____
	☐ _____ ☐ _____ ☐ _____
	☐ _____ ☐ _____ ☐ _____
	☐ _____ ☐ _____ ☐ _____
	☐ _____ ☐ _____ ☐ _____
	☐ _____ ☐ _____ ☐ _____
	☐ _____ ☐ _____ ☐ _____

my personal
Transition Appointment Reminder and To Do List

Date	Appointment / To Do's
	☐ _____ ☐ _____ ☐ _____
	☐ _____ ☐ _____ ☐ _____
	☐ _____ ☐ _____ ☐ _____
	☐ _____ ☐ _____ ☐ _____
	☐ _____ ☐ _____ ☐ _____
	☐ _____ ☐ _____ ☐ _____
	☐ _____ ☐ _____ ☐ _____

271

my personal
Transition Appointment
Reminder and To Do List

Date	Appointment / To Do's
	☐ _____
	☐ _____
	☐ _____
	☐ _____
	☐ _____
	☐ _____
	☐ _____
	☐ _____
	☐ _____
	☐ _____
	☐ _____
	☐ _____
	☐ _____
	☐ _____
	☐ _____
	☐ _____
	☐ _____
	☐ _____
	☐ _____
	☐ _____
	☐ _____

my personal
Transition Appointment Reminder and To Do List

Date	Appointment / To Do's

- [ ] _____
- [ ] _____
- [ ] _____

- [ ] _____
- [ ] _____
- [ ] _____

- [ ] _____
- [ ] _____
- [ ] _____

- [ ] _____
- [ ] _____
- [ ] _____

- [ ] _____
- [ ] _____
- [ ] _____

- [ ] _____
- [ ] _____
- [ ] _____

- [ ] _____
- [ ] _____
- [ ] _____

my personal
Transition Appointment
Reminder and To Do List

Date	Appointment / To Do's
	☐ _____ ☐ _____ ☐ _____
	☐ _____ ☐ _____ ☐ _____
	☐ _____ ☐ _____ ☐ _____
	☐ _____ ☐ _____ ☐ _____
	☐ _____ ☐ _____ ☐ _____
	☐ _____ ☐ _____ ☐ _____
	☐ _____ ☐ _____ ☐ _____

my personal
Transition Appointment
Reminder and To Do List

Date	Appointment / To Do's

☐ _____
☐ _____
☐ _____

☐ _____
☐ _____
☐ _____

☐ _____
☐ _____
☐ _____

☐ _____
☐ _____
☐ _____

☐ _____
☐ _____
☐ _____

☐ _____
☐ _____
☐ _____

☐ _____
☐ _____
☐ _____

275

my personal
Notes

Notes

Notes

Notes

Notes

Notes

Notes

Notes

Notes

Notes

Notes

Notes

Notes

Notes

Notes

Additional
Military Resources
for
Transition Assistance

Additional
Military Resources

Additional military resources offer very important value by providing extra support and solutions for transitioning service members.

- **Additional military resources act as a link to important tools and services:** By combining all available trusted options, service members can access reliable information quickly and efficiently, saving time and decreasing the stress of searching for answers on their own.

- **Additional military resources help to ensure assistance is relevant and actionable:** Whether it's veteran-focused job and educational opportunities, military-specific financial tools, or healthcare contacts, resources empower service members to purposefully take their next steps of their transition with confidence.

- **Additional military resources encourage action:** Service members are motivated to explore various opportunities, apply for various benefits, and seek community support when needed.

Additional
Military Resources
cont.

- **Additional military resources provide long-term value:** Service members have access to resources as they continue to navigate life after separation. This ensures they have the tools and support needed to address future challenges and opportunities.

- **Additional military resources act as a trusted safety net:** Service members are empowered with confidence which helps them to make their transition smoother and more successful.

Additional
Military Resources
URLs

- **Career Resources**
  - **Hire Heroes USA:** Provides free job search assistance to U.S. military members, veterans, and their spouses.
    ### Website:
    https://www.hireheroesusa.org/

  - **Military.com Jobs:** Offers a job board and career advice for veterans.
    ### Website:
    https://www.military.com/veteran-jobs

- **Financial Planning Resources**
  - **Military OneSource Financial Counseling:** Provides free financial counseling to service members and their families.
    ### Website:
    https://www.militaryonesource.mil/financial-legal/personal-finance/

- ○ **Thrift Savings Plan (TSP):** A retirement savings plan for federal employees and members of the uniformed services.
  ### Website:
  https://www.tsp.gov/

- • **Healthcare Resources**
  - ○ **TRICARE:** Health care program for uniformed service members, retirees, and their families.
    ### Website:
    https://www.tricare.mil/

  - ○ **VA Health Care:** Information on VA health care benefits and how to apply.
    ### Website:
    https://www.va.gov/health-care/

Additional
Military Resources
URLs
cont.

- **Family Support**
  - **Military OneSource Family and Relationships:** Resources to help military families navigate life events.
    ### Website:
    https://www.militaryonesource.mil/family-relationships/

  - **National Military Family Association:** Supports military families through advocacy and programs.
    ### Website:
    https://www.militaryfamily.org/

- **General Transition Help**
  - **Department of Veterans Affairs:** Official website that provides information on benefits, health care, and more.
    ### Website:
    https:///www.va.gov/

Additional MilitaryResources URLs
cont.

- American Legion: A veterans organization offering support and resources.

  Website:

  https:///www.legion.org/

Your Next Chapter

Your Next Chapter

Welcome to your next chapter, one that you've earned through dedication, sacrifice, and resilience. We honor not just the years you've given in service, but the profound impact you've made along the way. Your transition from active duty to veteran is more than a change in title, it is a transition to a place of honor within a proud community of those who have served. You now stand among those who will forever be part of the legacy of strength, loyalty, and courage that defines our great nation.

As you continue to move forward, know that your experiences, skills, and values remain as important as ever. Your discipline, leadership, and commitment will be lasting assets for you and those you influence. Now is your time to reflect on your accomplishments and look ahead to new opportunities and adventures —while remaining grounded in the same strength and resilience that carried you through every mission, challenge, and triumph.

**Cheers to
Your Next Chapter!**

Hello Veteran

Hello Veteran

Veteran, hello and welcome to a lifelong community that genuinely values your service and applauds your ongoing journey. This next chapter is yours to mold, and your contributions as a veteran hold powerful potential. It is an honor to walk beside you in this new season of your life, knowing that your legacy of military service will inspire generations to come.

Hello Veteran!

My Fellow Veterans

My fellow **Veterans,** it has been my pleasure and honor to serve alongside you during peacetime and wartime. I celebrate you with the acronym I created for **Veterans** symbolizing my admiration for your commitment, capturing the essence of who you are and the legacy you continue to uphold. Your unwavering dedication, sacrifice, and service represent the core values we live by every day.

Thank you for your service!
God Bless You! God Bless America!

VETERANS

VALOR: Infused in every step of the way. Your courage and bravery are woven into the very fabric of your service.

ENDURING: Unwavering resilience, unbroken spirit. You have faced every challenge with steadfast resolve, never wavering in your commitment.

TENACITY: Beyond boundaries and despite obstacles. Your relentless determination has allowed you to overcome even the greatest hardships.

EXEMPLIFYING: Honor and sacrifice. You set the highest standards through your honorable service, putting the needs of others before your own.

RESPECTED: Guardians, standing tall. You are the protectors of freedom, standing tall with pride and respect for the values you defend.

ADMIRABLE: Selfless service to country with bravery. Your willingness to serve selflessly, with courage and strength, inspires all who know your story.

NOBLE HEARTS: United and strong. Together, as one, you embody the heart and soul of our nation's resilience and spirit.

STEADFAST PATRIOTS: Defenders of liberty. You remain unwavering in your defense of the liberty and freedoms that define our great country.

my personal

Tribute Quotes to Service and Sacrifice

Department of Defense (DoD) and Military-Civilian Transition Office (MCTO)

"To those transitioning from uniform to new beginnings—Service does not end when the uniform comes off, it evolves. The Department of Defense, through the Military-Civilian Transition Office, remains steadfast in its mission to ensure every service member is equipped with the knowledge, resources, and support needed to thrive beyond the military. Your dedication, resilience, and leadership continue to shape the world, just as they did in service to this nation. **Your next mission awaits, step forward with confidence and purpose.**"

~ Dr. Sonya Howell Barrow

United States Army

"**To the Soldiers of the United States Army—**You have stood strong in the face of adversity, defended freedom across the globe, and served with unwavering honor. Your dedication to the mission, to your fellow Soldiers, and to the American people is the foundation upon which the Army's strength is built. As you transition into the next chapter of your journey, carry forward the discipline, leadership, and resilience that made you an indispensable force. Your service does not end with the uniform—it evolves into new opportunities to lead, inspire, and impact the world beyond the battlefield. **Thank you for your courage, sacrifice, and steadfast commitment. Hooah!**"

~ Dr. Sonya Howell Barrow
Chief Warrant Officer Five (CW5) - Retired
Combat Veteran

United States Navy

"To the Sailors of the United States Navy—Your courage and commitment have carried you across vast oceans, safeguarding our nation with strength and honor. Whether standing watch on the deck of a destroyer or operating in the quiet depths of a submarine, you have faced the unknown with steady hands and steadfast hearts. As you transition into civilian life, know that your discipline, adaptability, and devotion to service will continue to chart a successful course. The sea has taught you resilience, unity, and perseverance—qualities that will guide you through every new horizon. **Fair winds and following seas.**"

~ Dr. Sonya Howell Barrow

United States Air Force

"To the Airmen of the United States Air Force—You have soared through the skies with vigilance and valor, safeguarding our nation from above and advancing the frontiers of air and space superiority. Your service, sacrifice, and relentless innovation have shaped not only the mission, but the future. As you embark on your next journey beyond the uniform, know that the sky was never the limit—it was your launch point. The integrity, excellence, and resilience instilled in you by the Air Force will carry you confidently into whatever lies ahead. **Aim high—fly, fight, and win."**

~ Dr. Sonya Howell Barrow

United States Marine Corps

"To the Marines of the United States Marine Corps— You have answered the call with courage, forged through fire and tested by duty. From the shores of distant lands to the front lines of every fight, your honor, courage, and commitment have defined the essence of what it means to be a Marine. As you transition from active service, know that the values instilled in you—discipline, loyalty, and an unbreakable warrior spirit—will continue to lead you with purpose. **You may leave the Corps, but the Corps never leaves you. Semper Fidelis."**

~ Dr. Sonya Howell Barrow

United States Coast Guard

"To the Coast Guardsmen of the United States Coast Guard—You have braved the storm, stood watch on every coast, and safeguarded our nation's waters with vigilance, courage, and honor. Whether responding to disaster, enforcing maritime law, or rescuing those in peril, your dedication has saved lives and upheld security across every shore. As you transition beyond the uniform, may the discipline, adaptability, and selfless service that guided you at sea continue to navigate your journey ahead. **Thank you for your unwavering commitment to duty—Semper Paratus."**

~ Dr. Sonya Howell Barrow

United States Space Force

"To the Guardians of the United States Space Force— You stand at the forefront of a new frontier, securing the ultimate high ground with vigilance, innovation, and resolve. As defenders of space and stewards of tomorrow's technologies, your service marks a historic shift in how we protect and empower our nation. As you transition beyond the uniform, carry forward the clarity, adaptability, and pioneering spirit that define you as a Guardian. **Your journey doesn't end at the edge of space—it begins there. Semper Supra."**

~ Dr. Sonya Howell Barrow

National Guard

"**To the committed service members of the National Guard—**You live a dual life of devotion, answering the call of duty while remaining rooted in your communities. You are teachers, parents, first responders, neighbors—and soldiers. You show up for drill weekends, emergencies, deployments, and for your families in between. You've given your time, your energy, and your heart, often without recognition. As you move toward this new season, may you walk forward with the same courage that carried you through every mission. **Your path may be complex, but it is built on honor. You have served well. Now it's time to serve yourself—with purpose, peace, and pride.**"

~ Dr. Sonya Howell Barrow

Reserves

"To the dedicated warriors of the Reserve — Across every branch—Army, Navy, Air Force, Marines, Coast Guard—you've answered the call while managing the demands of civilian life. You trained in readiness, often on borrowed time, sacrificing weekends, holidays, and personal milestones to stay prepared for the unknown. You've mastered the art of dual service —balancing duty, work, and family with quiet resilience and unshakable dedication. As you transition into this next chapter, know that your sacrifice has meaning and your journey commands respect. Carry the discipline and determination that defined your service into this new mission: building a life you don't need to recover from. **You've done the work for others—now, it's time to pour that same energy into yourself."**

~ Dr. Sonya Howell Barrow

United States
Department of Labor (DOL)

"To the stewards of America's labor system—your unwavering commitment to protecting workers' rights, strengthening employment pathways, and advancing fair labor practices has been a guiding force behind economic progress. Your leadership in workforce development, job training, and equitable opportunity has uplifted millions and ensured a more inclusive and sustainable future of work. As you continue to champion the American worker, your legacy of advocacy, innovation, and integrity leaves a permanent mark on our nation's economic fabric. **Thank you for empowering the workforce and shaping policy that moves lives forward."**

~ Dr. Sonya Howell Barrow

United States Department of Veterans Affairs (VA)

"To the devoted professionals of the VA—your tireless work in caring for those who have worn the uniform is both noble and necessary. You serve not just with skill, but with compassion, providing a lifeline of healthcare, benefits, and hope to veterans and their families. Your dedication ensures that those who have sacrificed for our nation are never forgotten or left behind. In every clinic, claim, and counseling session, your impact is personal and profound. **Thank you for being a steadfast pillar of support to our heroes beyond their time in uniform.**"

~ Dr. Sonya Howell Barrow

Wounded Warrior Project (WWP)

"To the warriors who have faced adversity with strength, resilience, and an unbreakable spirit—
Your courage reaches far beyond the battlefield. Through every obstacle, you continue to rise, inspiring others and leading by example. The Wounded Warrior Project stands as a powerful testament to the enduring commitment to uplift, empower, and walk beside those who have sacrificed for this nation. As you move forward on your journey, know this: you are never alone. Your service matters. Your strength matters. Your story matters. Keep pressing on, embracing new possibilities, and proving—again and again—that no challenge is too great. **You are a warrior—today, tomorrow, and always.**"

~ Dr. Sonya Howell Barrow

my personal
Monthly Reminders

Year____

January
- ☐ _____
- ☐ _____
- ☐ _____
- ☐ _____
- ☐ _____
- ☐ _____
- ☐ _____

February
- ☐ _____
- ☐ _____
- ☐ _____
- ☐ _____
- ☐ _____
- ☐ _____
- ☐ _____

March
- ☐ _____
- ☐ _____
- ☐ _____
- ☐ _____
- ☐ _____
- ☐ _____
- ☐ _____

April
- ☐ _____
- ☐ _____
- ☐ _____
- ☐ _____
- ☐ _____
- ☐ _____
- ☐ _____

May
- ☐ _____
- ☐ _____
- ☐ _____
- ☐ _____
- ☐ _____
- ☐ _____
- ☐ _____

June
- ☐ _____
- ☐ _____
- ☐ _____
- ☐ _____
- ☐ _____
- ☐ _____
- ☐ _____

July
- ☐ _____
- ☐ _____
- ☐ _____
- ☐ _____
- ☐ _____
- ☐ _____
- ☐ _____

August
- ☐ _____
- ☐ _____
- ☐ _____
- ☐ _____
- ☐ _____
- ☐ _____
- ☐ _____

September
- ☐ _____
- ☐ _____
- ☐ _____
- ☐ _____
- ☐ _____
- ☐ _____
- ☐ _____

October
- ☐ _____
- ☐ _____
- ☐ _____
- ☐ _____
- ☐ _____
- ☐ _____
- ☐ _____

November
- ☐ _____
- ☐ _____
- ☐ _____
- ☐ _____
- ☐ _____
- ☐ _____
- ☐ _____

December
- ☐ _____
- ☐ _____
- ☐ _____
- ☐ _____
- ☐ _____
- ☐ _____
- ☐ _____

Year____

January
- [ ] _____
- [ ] _____
- [ ] _____
- [ ] _____
- [ ] _____
- [ ] _____
- [ ] _____

February
- [ ] _____
- [ ] _____
- [ ] _____
- [ ] _____
- [ ] _____
- [ ] _____
- [ ] _____

March
- [ ] _____
- [ ] _____
- [ ] _____
- [ ] _____
- [ ] _____
- [ ] _____
- [ ] _____

April
- [ ] _____
- [ ] _____
- [ ] _____
- [ ] _____
- [ ] _____
- [ ] _____
- [ ] _____

May
- [ ] _____
- [ ] _____
- [ ] _____
- [ ] _____
- [ ] _____
- [ ] _____
- [ ] _____

June
- [ ] _____
- [ ] _____
- [ ] _____
- [ ] _____
- [ ] _____
- [ ] _____
- [ ] _____

July
- [ ] _____
- [ ] _____
- [ ] _____
- [ ] _____
- [ ] _____
- [ ] _____
- [ ] _____

August
- [ ] _____
- [ ] _____
- [ ] _____
- [ ] _____
- [ ] _____
- [ ] _____
- [ ] _____

September
- [ ] _____
- [ ] _____
- [ ] _____
- [ ] _____
- [ ] _____
- [ ] _____
- [ ] _____

October
- [ ] _____
- [ ] _____
- [ ] _____
- [ ] _____
- [ ] _____
- [ ] _____
- [ ] _____

November
- [ ] _____
- [ ] _____
- [ ] _____
- [ ] _____
- [ ] _____
- [ ] _____
- [ ] _____

December
- [ ] _____
- [ ] _____
- [ ] _____
- [ ] _____
- [ ] _____
- [ ] _____
- [ ] _____

my personal

Countdown
to
Transition
~
Notebook
and Planner
for
Non-Retiring
Service Members

By International Best-Selling Author

United States Army
Chief Warrant Officer Five (CW5) - Retired
Combat Veteran

Dr. Sonya Howell Barrow

About The Author

Dr. Sonya Howell Barrow

Dr. Sonya Howell Barrow is a retired U.S. Army Combat Veteran who served honorably and distinctively for over 26+ years in various organizations and deployments before medically retiring as a Chief Warrant Officer Five (CW5) in November 2018. She was born at Fort Gordon (previously known as Camp Gordon, now known as Fort Eisenhower), Georgia and raised between Augusta and Warrenton, Georgia. She is a mother of two adult sons, Jacques and DeShon Jr.

Dr. Sonya received her Doctor of Humane Letters from Mainseed Christian University (MCU) and achieved the credentials of Global Fellowship in Leadership Principles. As an Information Technology and Cyber Security professional, she earned her Master's Degree in Cyber Security from the University of Maryland, University College (now known as University of Maryland Global Campus).

Since her retirement from the U.S. Army, Dr. Sonya has pursued her dream as a published author. She is an

Amazon International Bestselling Author, Certified Life Coach, Founder of AuthorpreneurSonya, CEO and Owner of The SoJaDe Group, LLC and SoJaDe Publishing, LLC.

If Dr. Sonya isn't reading, traveling, and spending time with family and friends, she is writing and motivating others by letting them know that the "glass is always half full, never half empty." With her faith, strong will, and determination, she chooses to be a beacon of hope and strives to encourage others to live their best lives that are filled with confidence, self-awareness, and personal growth. Dr. Sonya provides a creative artistic space via her social media platforms and websites to showcase her non-fiction and fiction published works spanning across four distinct genres:

1-Inspire and Motivate: **Fearless. Inspired. Resilient. Empowered. - 🔥FIRE.**

2-Self-Help: **Growth. Leadership. Elevation. - 🍌 GLE.**

3-Soldier Girl: **Military Life.**

4-Entertainment: **Tantalizing. Enchanting. Ascending. - ☕ TEA.**

With a diverse collection spanning across four genres, Dr. Sonya invite readers into a world of inspiration, insight, and adventure. Each published work is a testament to her passion for storytelling, delivered thoughtfully and authentically.

Igniting Your 🔥FIRE.
Encouraging Your 🐒 GLE.
Savoring My ☕ TEA.

"Inspiring, motivating, encouraging, and entertaining readers through captivating storytelling by telling one story at a time."

~ Dr. Sonya Howell Barrow

Contact Information

Contact Information

Email:
hello@sonyahowellbarrow.com

Website:
http://www.sonyahowellbarrow.com

Linktr.ee:
https://linktr.ee/sonyahowellbarrow

Facebook:
https://www.facebook.com/authorpreneursonya

Instagram:
https://www.instagram.com/authorpreneursonya

LinkedIn:
https://www.linkedin.com/in/sonyahowellbarrow/

Amazon Author Central:
https://www.amazon.com/stores/Sonya-Howell-Barrow/author/B0C5425D8W?

DR. SONYA HOWELL BARROW

335

www.ingramcontent.com/pod-product-compliance
Lightning Source LLC
Chambersburg PA
CBHW071706120626
46550CB00001B/125